THE LEGEND OF ZELDA

BY JARIYA GOERWITZ

EPIC

BELLWETHER MEDIA ♦ MINNEAPOLIS, MN

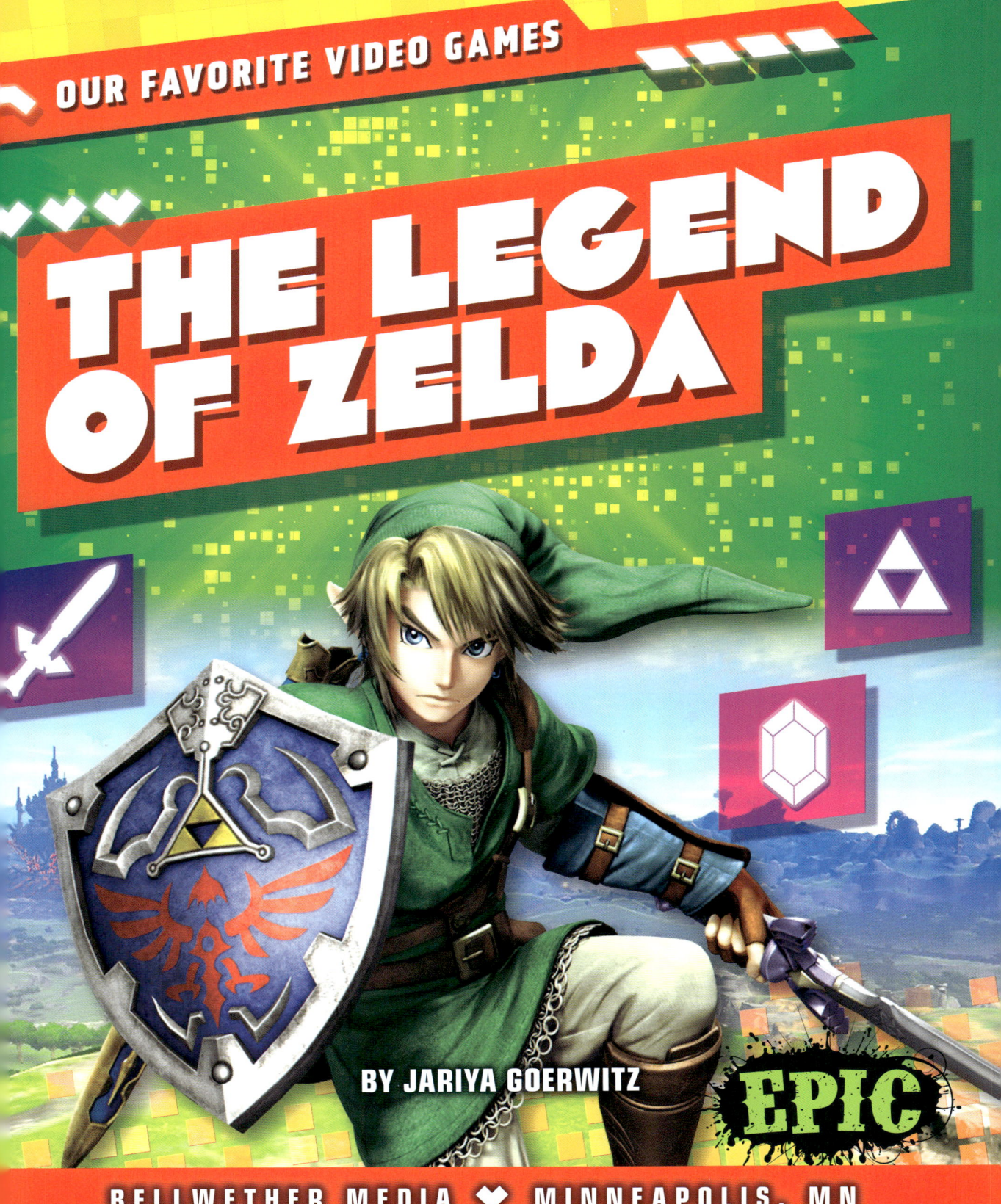

EPIC

EPIC BOOKS are no ordinary books. They burst with intense action, high-speed heroics, and shadows of the unknown. Are you ready for an Epic adventure?

This edition first published in 2025 by Bellwether Media, Inc.

Library of Congress Cataloging-in-Publication Data

Names: Goerwitz, Jariya, author.
Title: The Legend of Zelda / by Jariya Goerwitz.
Description: Minneapolis, MN : Bellwether Media, 2025. | Series: Epic. Our favorite video games | Includes bibliographical references and index. | Audience: Ages 7-12 | Audience: Grades 2-3 | Summary: "Engaging images accompany information about The Legend of Zelda. The combination of high-interest subject matter and light text is intended for students in grades 2 through 7"-- Provided by publisher.
Identifiers: LCCN 2024005411 (print) | LCCN 2024005412 (ebook) | ISBN 9798893040463 (library binding) | ISBN 9781644879863 (ebook)
Subjects: LCSH: Legend of Zelda (Game)--Juvenile literature.
Classification: LCC GV1469.35.L43 G64 2025 (print) | LCC GV1469.35.L43 (ebook) | DDC 794.8--dc23/eng/20240205
LC record available at https://lccn.loc.gov/2024005411
LC ebook record available at https://lccn.loc.gov/2024005412

Editor: Elizabeth Neuenfeldt   Designer: Gabriel Hilger

Printed in the United States of America, North Mankato, MN.

TABLE OF CONTENTS

000
HIGH SCORE

FLYING HIGH

A player controls Link in *Tears of the Kingdom*. They need to cross a wide gap.

The player takes out a fan. They take out a wing. They make an airplane. Now they can cross!

TEARS OF THE KINGDOM

A Control

5

The Legend of Zelda is a series of **action-adventure games**.

The games follow Link. He fights to save Princess Zelda and the land of Hyrule. Players solve puzzles. They fight monsters!

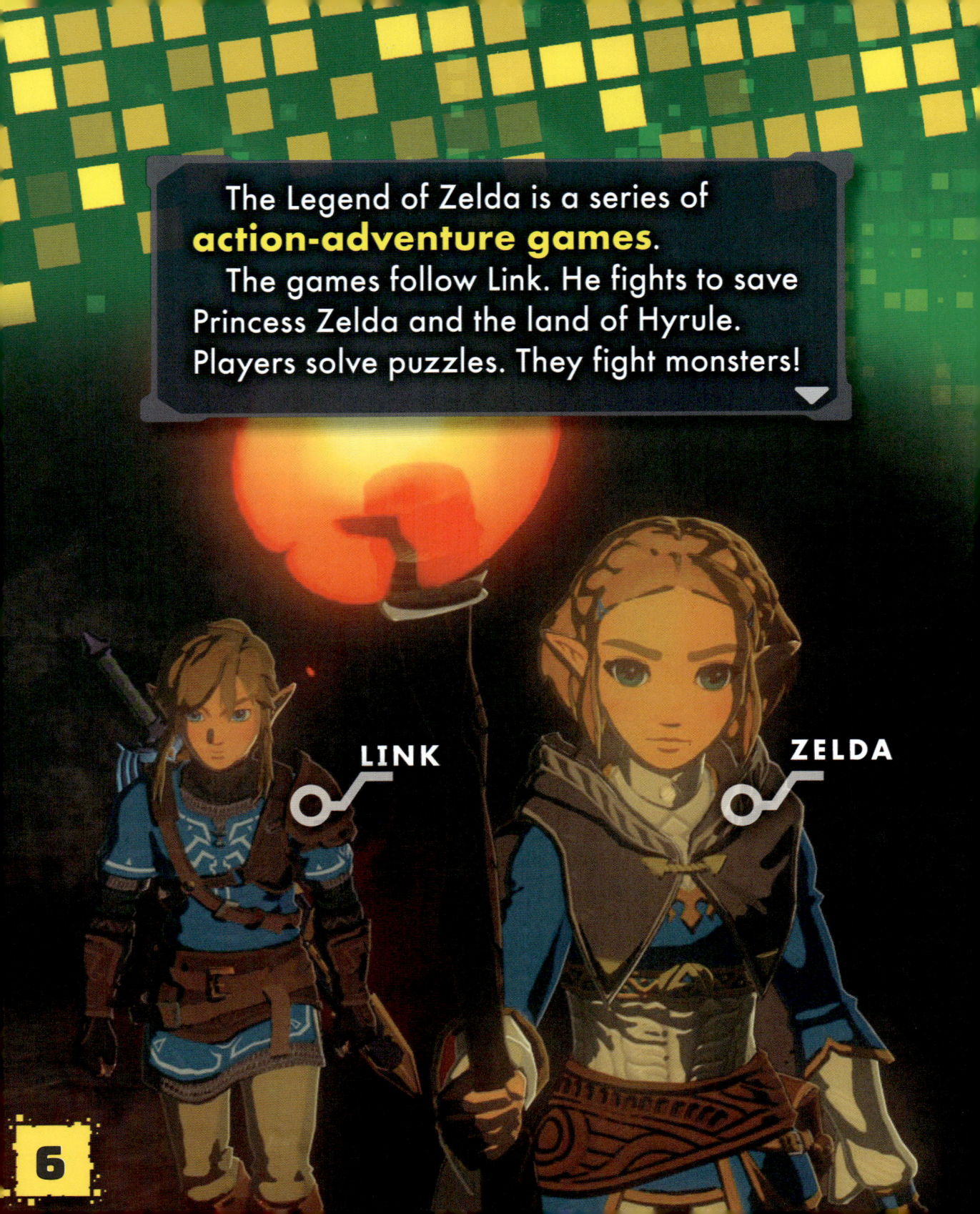

LINK

ZELDA

CHUCHU

BOKOBLIN

LYNEL

MOLDUGA

GANONDORF

KEESE

THE HISTORY OF THE LEGEND OF ZELDA

The Legend of Zelda was first made by Nintendo. This game came out in Japan in 1986.

THE LEGEND OF ZELDA

FIRST SAVE

The Legend of Zelda was the first video game to let players save their game.

> It came to the United States in 1987. It was played on the Nintendo Entertainment System.

NINTENDO ENTERTAINMENT SYSTEM

DEVELOPER PROFILE

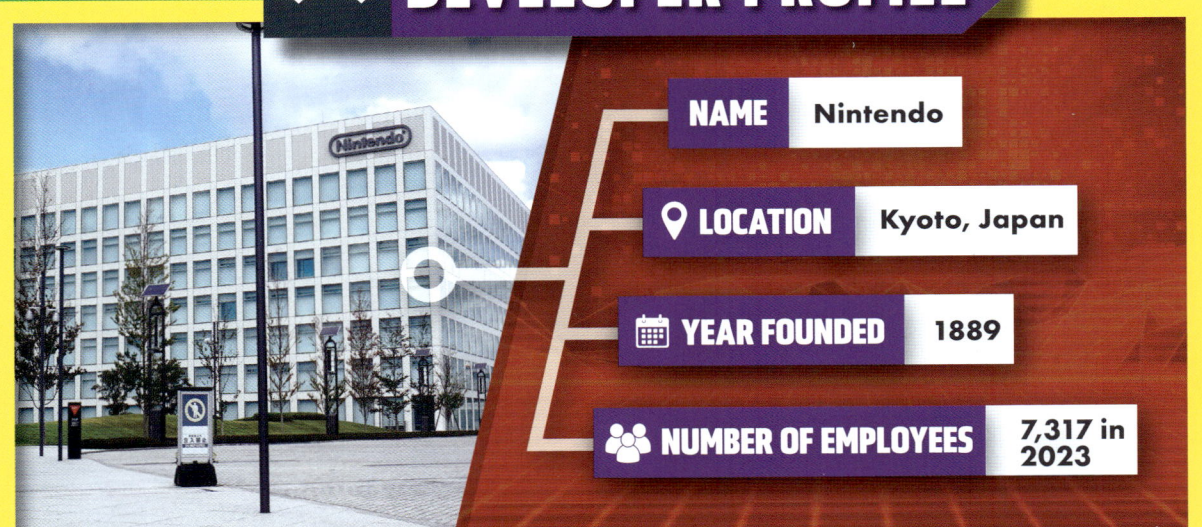

NAME	Nintendo
📍 **LOCATION**	Kyoto, Japan
📅 **YEAR FOUNDED**	1889
👥 **NUMBER OF EMPLOYEES**	7,317 in 2023

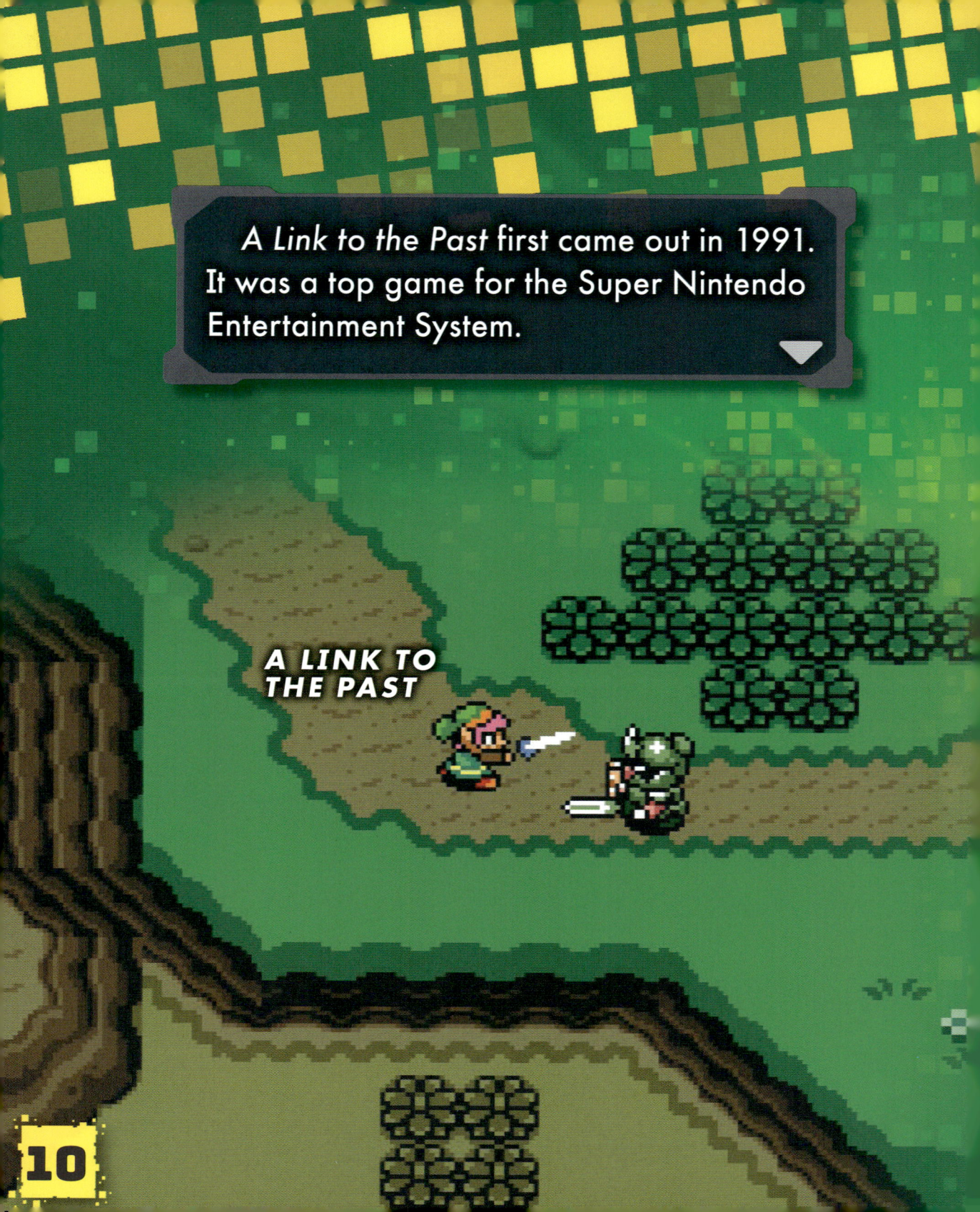

A *Link to the Past* first came out in 1991. It was a top game for the Super Nintendo Entertainment System.

A LINK TO THE PAST

OLD AND NEW

Nintendo remade *Link's Awakening*. The new game came out in 2019. It sold more than 6 million copies!

LINK'S AWAKENING

Link's Awakening was made for the Game Boy two years later. It was the first Zelda game for a handheld **console**.

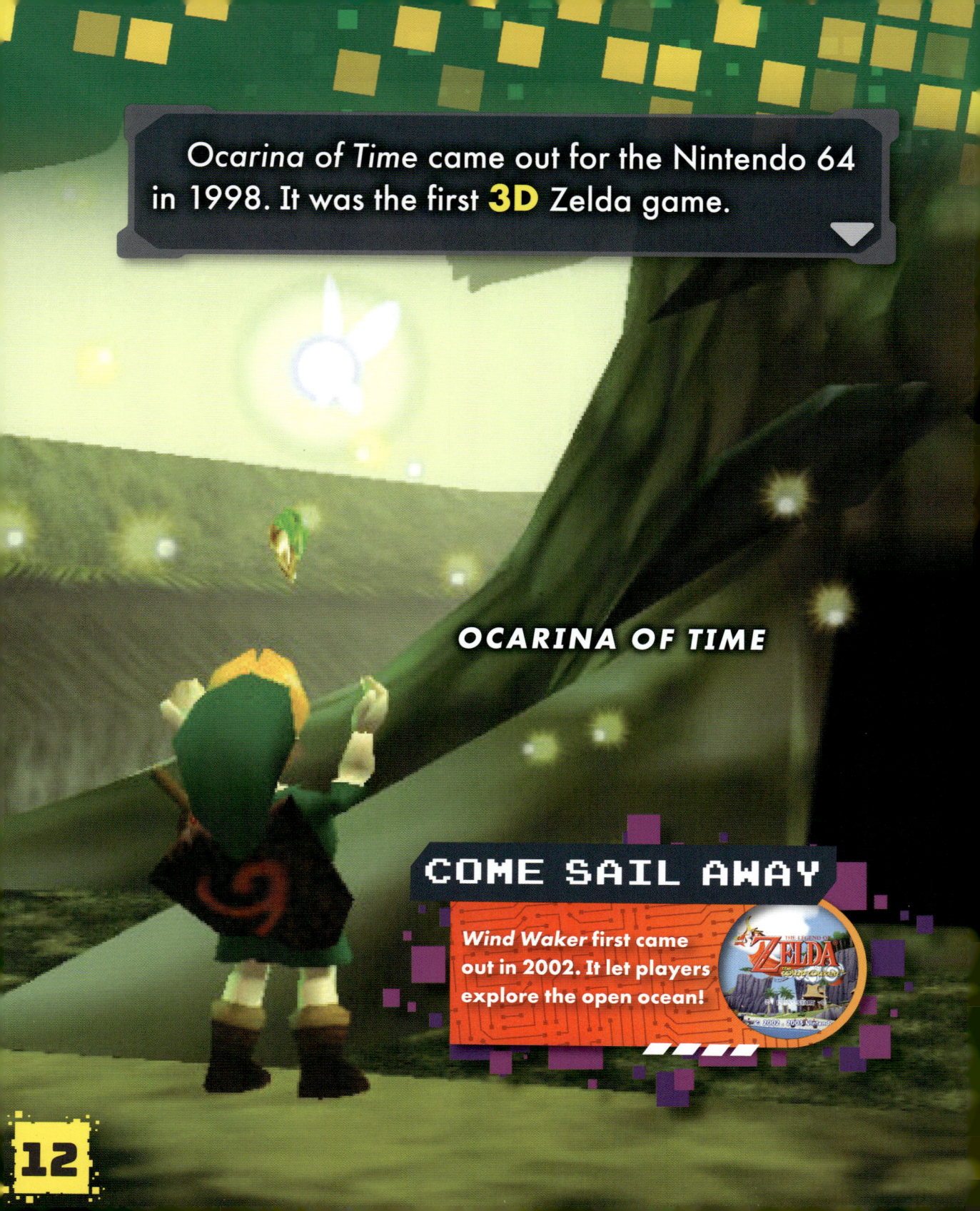

> Ocarina of Time came out for the Nintendo 64 in 1998. It was the first **3D** Zelda game.

OCARINA OF TIME

COME SAIL AWAY

Wind Waker first came out in 2002. It let players explore the open ocean!

In 2013, *A Link Between Worlds* came out on the Nintendo 3DS. This **2D** game was a hit!

TEARS OF THE KINGDOM

Breath of the Wild was released for the Nintendo Switch in 2017. It was the first **open-world** Zelda game.

Tears of the Kingdom came out in 2023. It let players explore floating islands!

14

THE LEGEND OF ZELDA TIMELINE

1986
The Legend of Zelda game comes out in Japan

1993
Link's Awakening is the first Zelda game on a handheld console

1998
Ocarina of Time is the first 3D Zelda game

2017
Breath of the Wild is the first open-world game in the series

2023
Tears of the Kingdom comes out

THE LEGEND OF ZELDA TODAY

There are more than 40 Zelda games. Fans play on consoles.

They explore open worlds in 3D Zelda games. They travel through **top-down** worlds in 2D Zelda games.

THE LEGEND OF ZELDA FANS

The series has grown beyond games. Writers tell the story in books. People collect toys and other items.

THE LEGEND OF ZELDA GAMES BY SALES

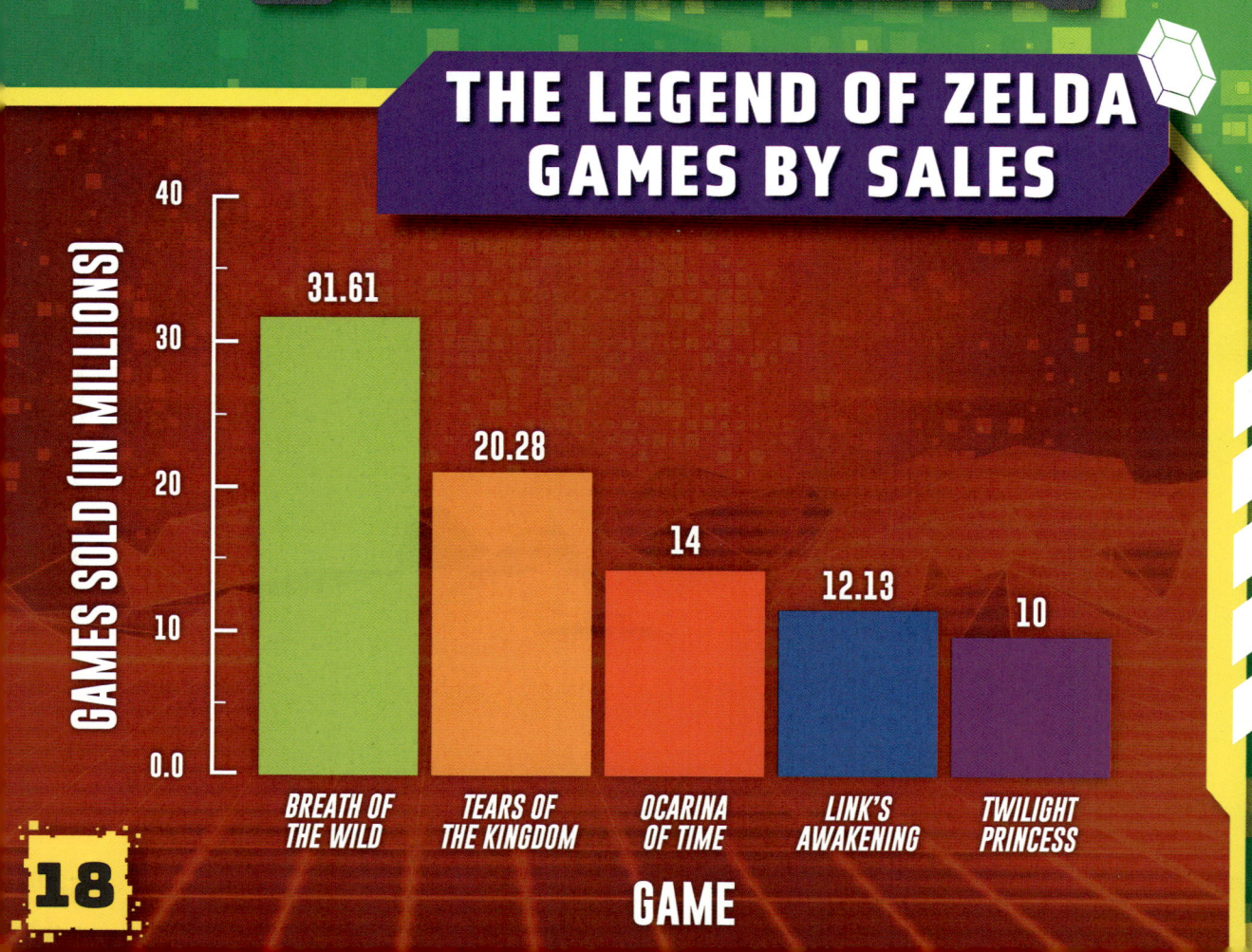

GAMES SOLD (IN MILLIONS)

- 40
- 30
- 20
- 10
- 0.0

- BREATH OF THE WILD — 31.61
- TEARS OF THE KINGDOM — 20.28
- OCARINA OF TIME — 14
- LINK'S AWAKENING — 12.13
- TWILIGHT PRINCESS — 10

GAME

In 2023, a movie of the series was announced.

Fans of Zelda games go to **conventions**. Some fans **cosplay** as their favorite characters! Other fans do **speedruns**. They want to see who can finish games the fastest. People love the Legend of Zelda!

ZELDATHON

DATE	about twice a year
LOCATION	online

EVENT

an online event where fans play Zelda games to raise money for different causes

GLOSSARY

2D—related to something that has height and width; players can only move left, right, up, or down in a 2D game.

3D—related to something that has height, width, and depth; players can move in any direction in a 3D game.

action-adventure games—games that involve exploring, solving puzzles, talking to characters, climbing, and fighting

console—a game system that connects to a screen to play video games; handheld consoles have a built-in screen.

conventions—events where fans of a subject meet

cosplay—to dress up as a character

open-world—related to a type of game where players explore a wide area at their own pace

speedruns—timed playthroughs of video games in which players finish the game as quickly as possible

top-down—related to a camera angle that shows the game's setting and the player from above

TO LEARN MORE

AT THE LIBRARY

Abdo, Kenny. *Link: Legend of Zelda Hero.* Mendota Heights, Minn.: North Star Editions, 2020.

Downs, Kieran. *Super Mario Bros.* Minneapolis, Minn.: Bellwether Media, 2025.

Rathburn, Betsy. *Video Game Developer.* Minneapolis, Minn.: Bellwether Media, 2023.

ON THE WEB

FACTSURFER

Factsurfer.com gives you a safe, fun way to find more information.

1. Go to www.factsurfer.com.

2. Enter "The Legend of Zelda" into the search box and click Q.

3. Select your book cover to see a list of related content.

INDEX